Favor The Odds

Dysfunction to Dynamic

Nakia Boglin

Copyright © 2019 Nakia Boglin. All rights reserved. No part of this book can be reproduced in any form without the written permission of the author and its publisher

Table of Contents

Introduction 9

Finding A Better Life...11

Being A Single Mom 17

Doing Things On My Own 23

Fruit Of Determination......................................25

Gone Too Soon..29

Searching For Balance In The Aftermath 35

Moving Back To Chaos 39

Reclaiming My life...43

Take Responsibility 47

Keep The Faith 51

Keep Moving Forward.......................................55

Show Up And Do The Work 61

Learn From The Giants......................................65

Have The Right Mindset....................................69

Giving Back..73

Fulfill Your Purpose And Your Destiny 77

Introduction

Everything you are going through right now is for a reason and a purpose.

There are times in our lives where it feels like all the odds are against us, or it feels like we are the odds. We are the person or outcast who just do not fit in. During these times, it easy to buy into the message that we are not enough. But that is not true. The true message is that there is a reason behind everything that you are going through right now. It is building character and perseverance for the greatness ahead.

Sometimes it may be hard to see that in the midst of where you are right now. But I promise you, everything has a purpose, it is for a reason, and in the end, it is going to be in your favor because the odds are not stacked against you. The odds are in your favor.

Finding A Better Life

I have spent a lot of years working in the Real Estate Industry as a broker and investor. I am licensed in three states and have a twenty year-old-son. Things in my life are working out better than I would have imagined at one point. I know now that everything I went through was leading me to where I am now. But it has not always been that way.

I grew up in a very dysfunctional house. The relationships I witnessed growing up were not based on honesty, respect, freedom or trust. The relationships were based on manipulation, betrayal, violence, and dysfunction. My four brothers were in and out of prison and jail. My mom and dad had an extremely abusive and toxic relationship. When my parents divorced, I was eleven. My mother got custody of me.

I remember when I was living with my mother, I would get out of school at three o'clock I would catch the bus or walk six miles to the area we moved to which was where my mother grew up, my grandparent's old house. I would sit outside until about twelve am because I didn't have a key. My mother worked second shift from three pm to eleven pm. Someday after school, I would go to the library until it closed then I would walk home. After a while, I started meeting people around the neighborhood hanging out, it gave me something to do until my mother got home from work. I remember telling my father about this. I would move back and forth between my mother and father. I was being pulled in every direction because my parents were in the aftermath of their divorce, which intensified feelings, anger and toxic patterns in the relationship they had with each other for many years. It felt like I got lost in the chaos of their divorce because I was the youngest child and only girl.

When I was thirteen years old, my mom kicked me out of the house. I went to live with one of my brothers for a while. I stay with him until his life challenges started to spill over into the relationships around him. I moved in with my father until my mother demanded I come back to live with her because my dad asked her for the child support, he was paying her to be spent on me since I was living with him at that time. Being that my mom had custody, I moved back with my mom. After a while, my mom kicked me out again before I was fourteen years old, a pattern that would continue for years.

Being A Single Mom

At the age of fourteen, I found out I was pregnant. Being pregnant, I could not continue at the high school I was enrolled in after I reached 6months because the school could only excuse so many absences for my Doctor appointments. Having so many absences would count against my attendance record. I would not be able to stay enrolled. I found a high school in the city that had a program for young mothers. However, this school was out of my district. I had to walk five miles to school because I did not have any money to ride public transportation. After a while, one of my teachers was kind and helpful; she would pick me up in the mornings for school. She was such a huge blessing to me. This school allowed me to make up some classes so I could go to my doctor's appointments without it counting against me. This way I could stay in school. After I gave birth, the school also had a nursery with staff to care for my son when I attended classes. I could check on him as much as I wanted. This was such a blessing to have this school, nursery, and people who helped me because my son's father was in prison.

As a teenage single mom, I had to take responsibility and provide for my son. I applied for a work permit and begin working at fifteen years old. My dad would pick Baron up from the school nursey and take him to the babysitter. I would leave school and walk to work. I wanted everything else to be better for Baron even at that moment as a teenager. I wanted him to have a better life than I had. I cannot say I started making all the perfect choices because I still encountered a lot of challenges. Within a year time, I was pregnant again. This time my mom helped me by keeping Baron while I attended school. I enrolled in another high school closer to my mom. This was the third high school I attended. It did not take long before my mom decides to kick me out again. After I gave birth to my daughter Jakia, my strained relationship with my mother got worse.

Jakia's father did not assist me with supporting her. At seventeen years old I found myself staying in a hotel with my two kids rather than allowing this to become a defining moment that held me down, it became the situation that made me realize I had to find something better. I had to move out and up from the situation that I was living in. I went to live with a family friend who was like a brother to me, He and his wife allowed me to stay a while to get myself together.

Doing Things On My Own

I started to focus on myself. I got clear on the distractions in my life and replaced distractions with goals. I created goals I wanted to achieve. I found a job and finally I got my own apartment. I moved about thirty miles away from my family and friends. I realized I needed to make more healthy and productive choices in my life. I enrolled in a community college and started working a second job. I did not have a car, so I would walk about three miles to the daycare, from the daycare I would call a taxi so my kids would not have to walk so far home. My mom and stepfather moved closer to me. They would pick the kids up some days. Eventually, the same toxic patterns from my mom and my relationship started to reappear.

Fruit Of Determination

I despised where I was more than I feared where I was going. In order to grow, one thing was clear to me. That was, I had to leave Alabama, the environment was chaotic and stagnate. I saved enough money. So, at eighteen years old Baron, Jakia, and I moved from Alabama to Atlanta. I wanted a change. I wanted to give my kids an opportunity to see and experience something different than what I seen growing up.

However, moving to Georgia posed challenges of its own. Life seems to be better than how it used to be back in Alabama. I found a job at a bank. I started learning new things and meeting different people from different walks of life, which enhance my views, boundaries, values, and beliefs. It prompted me to learn various things and set different goals than I could have imagined. I enrolled in another college. I would find free self-improvement or job training courses. I would attend. I would take the kids to the library. We would check out books and read together as a family. The kids were excelling in school, and I was finally able to see growth in myself and to see my kids experience a healthy and stable home.

At the age of twenty-three, I purchased my first home, I had learned about home ownership and credit from some of the courses I attended and from books I read, finally our own home. I loved the amazing feeling I got when I would hear Baron and Jakia pattering feet running through the house or even just watching them play in the yard while I was taking online courses. Everything seemed perfect until it wasn't, something terrible happened.

Gone Too Soon

Three weeks before Thanksgiving, we celebrated Jakia's seventh birthday at Chuck E Cheese, she had so much fun. She said, "This is the best birthday ever!" little did we know that it would be her last birthday celebration.

My mother had come to visit for the holiday and Jakia was so excited to see her because Jakia had been asking for my mom to visit for some time. About two days before Thanksgiving, Jakia had a headache. I took her to the hospital, where she was seen and released. When we got home, I put her to bed so she could get some rest. When she was asleep, I began baking pies for the holiday. The next morning as I begin to make breakfast. I notice little fingerprints on one sweet potato pies. I knew right away they belong to Jakia. I called Jakia to ask her about the fingerprints in the pies she said: "of course they are my fingerprints mommy I came downstairs last night when everyone was asleep because I didn't get a chance to lick the spoon." She said she needed to taste the pie to make sure I had mixed it right. Jakia and Baron would often lick the spoon that I used for mixing every time I baked pies. I told them they were my food critics, after all. They were really honest about how my cooking tasted.

Later that night, Jakia was not feeling well again, so I took her back to the hospital. Who would have a guessed that within twenty hours she would be gone? My family and friends came to the hospital after finding out what happened. I was so confused. I could not understand what was happening. How could this happen? My precious seven-year-old daughter was gone.

This was the most excruciating pain I had ever had to endure. My life seemed to have stopped; it felt like life grabbed me by my ankles and turned me upside down. I had no balance, my world seemed so blurred nothing made sense to me. This felt so out of order. I couldn't comprehend it. I believed the natural order was children were to bury their parents, not parents burying their kids. It went against the natural order of what I believed. I knew I had lost a part of my future that I would never get to see. I would never get a chance to see her attend high school, prom, graduation, or college. To be married and have children. A part of my future had evaded me.

Being a single mom with no support from either child's father. I had to plan her funeral and go back to work to make sure I could support Baron and myself. It was a roller coaster ride, especially because I didn't have anybody around to help because all of my family was back in Alabama.

I would cry and read the bible every night that's how I fell asleep. I had so many starts, stops, ups and downs, but I chose to remain prayerful in the midst of this. I could have never imagined this happening to me.

But I knew that I didn't have the choice to give up. Giving up or quitting was not an option for me. I had to keep working because I still had another child to provide for. It felt like I had no time to grieve. I had no support. I had not seen my family in a year, since the Christmas following Jakia's death.

It was just Baron and me on our own.

Later, I got laid off from my job as a Real Estate Title Examiner. I went through a struggle with keeping my home, so I started working several temporary jobs. Still, the income wasn't constant. I became delinquent in the mortgage payments my home went into foreclosure. At that time, it felt like everything was working against me.

Searching For Balance In The Aftermath

After the foreclosure, Baron and I moved into an apartment. That is when I started learning and researching about forbearance, short sales, and foreclosures. But I wanted to learn where I went wrong or what I could have done differently in my own experience so I and gathered all the experience and knowledge I had. I begin to understand the foreclosure process and industry. I enrolled in a real estate course, I took my test passed and got my Real Estate license. It wasn't the traditional way that some people learn to become real estate agents,

At twenty-five, I sold my first home. Starting in the real estate business allowed me to have more quality time with Baron, especially since we didn't have family around, and especially since we both had experienced a great loss. I would take him with me to the office and preview homes. He was my little assistant. Just getting started into Real Estate It wasn't enough money so I would work part-time at the banks in the evening and Saturday mornings. Baron would stay with friends while I worked. Sunday was the day Baron got to do the thing he wanted. All my attention was on him.

Moving Back To Chaos

I continue to take classes to elevate in the business, then the real estate market crashed the recession hit. I started working several temporary jobs. One day I get a call from my mom in Alabama telling me she had a stroke at this point it was her second stroke. My mom mentioned that this wasn't looking upward for her, she asked if I would come home expecting she had a short time to live. I went back to Alabama to care for my mom during the week and I would go back to Atlanta on the weekend since I was between jobs.

I needed to find more permanent employment, one day in Alabama I saw someone I worked with at my first banking job, which informed me of opening at the bank.

I called my previous supervisor who was still with the company I did an interview, and I was hired. I begin working, I took online courses to enhance my knowledge so I could advance to other positions. I was then hired as a foreclosure specialist. I had been working so much and had no time to go back to Atlanta on the weekends. I eventually moved from my apartment in Atlanta and put my things in storage.

Two weeks after I gave up my apartment, my mom came to me and said I had to leave. I packed up my son and left. I took him to a friend's house, and I sleep in my car. I begin to reflect on my actions, what I had done to be in this position again. What I had done previously to get out.

Reclaiming My life

I refocused and begin working twelve to sixteen hours daily so I could save money to move back to Atlanta. I had saved up six months of living expenses. I resigned from the bank. I moved back to Atlanta I started back into Real Estate. Then I was able to purchase a home within sixty days. This was home for us.

Soon I begin to see that my determination was having an impact. Baron was excelling in school again he graduated and enrolled in college.

I begin to realize that I was seeing the odds work in my favor, my reason for taking the risk of moving to another state, learning new things and staying dedicated to my goals for a better life. The determination turned into reality. Life got better and better. Even with these obstacles, I realized that I was learning things from what I was going through. I learned to forgive and release some relationships in order to grow and embrace new ones. I learned you can love people who are not good for you or have your best interested in mind or heart. I use to fell a sense of obligation to work on the relationships I had a required closeness to, I no longer feel that way. It's become clear to distance yourself from toxicity and negativity. I decided to cut my losses and work on my healing and growth.

Sometimes we can be in a place looking at things the wrong way. Most of my stress came from the way I respond to where I was. I took control of my life and lived on my own terms. I realized it was not my responsibility to detox toxic people, it was my responsibility to detox and detach myself from the part of me that resonated with their toxicity. I started to understand that God was creating a place and position for me. I realized all the times I thought I was struggling; I was actually transitioning.

Take Responsibility

I have accepted my past, I own it. Acceptance propels us forward. I cannot change my past, but I can use the experience and knowledge for the present and future. I made a commitment to myself that out of respect for my present and future, I release all the past people, places, thoughts, hurts, beliefs, and Patterns that do not serve me going forward. I release anything and anyone who was not essential to my growth. All the unhealthy energy and threads connected to my past I released. I have learned life is a process of releasing and surrendering. I have come to recognize there are many ways to release and surrender. I choose to refocus on my happiness, healing & growth.

You will be amazed at what you attract after you start believing in what you deserve. Speak what you seek until you see what you said, come to fruition. Focus on the positive things you desire, and slowly, they will become the things you start to see.

What I learned about taking responsibility for my life is, it is my life. No one can live my life it but me, accountability has been key for me, I hold my self accountable for my own happiness. This is my life. I get the opportunity to make myself happy. I am the person responsible for showing up for myself every day. I got clear on my needs and wants. Neglecting my needs and wants is not a clear way to show self-love. I wrote down my needs and wants and give attention to it. It is one of the ways I love myself.

Keep The Faith

I still, will have challenges and obstacles to face moving forward. I embrace the lessons that are given to me. I cannot tell God how to train me for the purpose I was created in this world. I get to show up listen, learn, and implement what life is preparing me for. I encourage you to see the opportunity to be open and available to greater. Encourage yourself.

Give yourself time. It means you take each situation as it comes and not see it as an end but see it as an opportunity. Use it as an opportunity for you to persevere and achieve something great. It is important that you keep the faith. Know that through prayer and seeking God that this moment that you are going through is just a lesson and that the odds are not against you and you are in favor even at this moment. Have faith in the new challenges, from the victory in the old challenges. God supply's all our needs.

God is looking for people with a level of Faith, confidence, and whose heart is set on him to show up and support them.

Many are called, but few are chosen. (Matthew 22:14) God has chosen you for such a time as this.

One of the things that I have learned is that hurt brings much awareness. As we embrace the things that have happened in our lives and acknowledge hurt and pain, we can then begin to see beyond those hurts to the lesson that can be learned from it. It's in that opportunity that we can begin to see the areas that we need to work on ourselves. My mind, heart, and spirit are transformed and renewed.

Keep Moving Forward

Today I encourage you to look for the opportunity to see the odds and the difference of what's on the surface, believe things are getting better no matter what is happening around you. Look deep within to see what you are feeling and hearing from your center and inner wisdom. Be still and listen. A quiet mind is the foundation of inner peace. Get still find your voice and let your inner wisdom guide you. For every loss there is a gain, for every gain there is a lesson, for every lesson there will be a Catalyst, Catalyst is a change for growth. As you learn to favor the odds, you will see it is you who will choose a different way of living. You can see a different outcome than those around you. It is available to them too, but you can't choose it for them. However, you can choose it for yourself.

Don't be afraid to make a mistake doing something, and getting it wrong is better than doing nothing. This is how we learn and grow. We will all make mistakes the important thing, do not cling to your mistake or allow it to be the defining factor. Learn the lesson. Once you release all that does not serve you, it can bring the very blessing you need. Every success has a trail of failure behind it. Every failure leads towards success. Celebrate your success and your failures. Those specific failures will become keys to help achieve your success. A quote by Winston Churchill states Success is the ability to go from one failure to another without losing enthusiasm. Success is not final, failure is not fatal: it is the courage to continue that counts. Every successful person has a painful story, every painful story has a successful ending.

People will not always agree with your ideas or dreams because the vision is yours. I believe we are all given unique dreams and ideas because it is a part of us that is divine and designed for us. Get busy living your life and fulfilling your dreams. (James 4:14) Who knows what tomorrow may bring, life is like a mist that appears for a little time then vanishes. Life is short, spend it with people who make you feel loved and make you laugh.

The latter days of your past are gone, and there is greater in your future. Keep going in spite of everything that is going on around you. Don't listen to the negative chatter around you let it go in one ear and the other, do not give negativity a place to dwell. I believe that you are on your way. Know that everything is working out. You have the strength and courage to push through. Know that through faith things are going to work out. All things are working for the good. (Romans 8:28)

What I learned about moving forward is at times I may be alone to shed the things that do not serve me. It is also a way to hear, see, and learn things I might not receive by being in the company of others. I learned that I was willing to put more commitment into pressing forward than others. I could not afford to be stuck. When I made a commitment to myself, my awareness of the endurance I gained became ever so present.

Show Up And Do The Work

My journey to this point in my life has not been the traditional way. All I need to do is show up, and then after I am there, do the work and follow through. I notice most time people get lost in the process because they do not follow through. Make a commitment to yourself, that you will become the best you that you can, that you will show up for yourself. Hold yourself accountable, so that you will stick with your dreams and goals.

I remember looking around at one point knowing that I was doing the right things and bad things seem to happen. Through the process, I was to embrace the hurt and challenges to understand that it was a chance to go through this hardship and to see why things were happening. I chose not to focus on the bad things but to favor the Positive things. It was an opportunity to learn things like patience, understanding, and resilience.

The more I showed up for myself, the less attention I gave to the dysfunction going on around me, the new things I discovered slowly started to replace the dysfunction that was always present. It allowed me to go from dysfunction to dynamic.

Although there may not be people there to help you through this hardship that you are going through right now, know there is a higher calling that you are called for and you will come through this moment and move to bigger and a brighter opportunity that God has for you.

When I showed up and started doing the work, this experience challenges my old ways of doing things. Every time I am tempted to react the old way, I remember I am not a hostage of my past, I am orchestrating my future. I forgive myself for things I didn't know at the time. No matter how difficult it is, I continue to follow through. Always be honest with yourself. Be yourself flaws and all, don't worry about what you been through focus on where you are going. Don't hide the flaws that make you unique. Who you are is a blessing. You have a blessing with your name on it, you have no idea how amazing it will be.

Learn From The Giants

There are times I notice people stay in comfort because they are afraid. In order to play big in your life, you must be willing to learn from the people who have been through what you are going through. Be willing to learn and play with giants don't be shy, feel small or out of place. Feeling shy, out of place, or small are only temporary, if you should you ever feel small let it be because you are looking at a bigger picture, a picture that is bigger than you ever imagined. Know that you have a purpose that you and only you can fulfill. Start to be aware of how you feel and why you feel this way. Sometimes if we are unaware of our feelings, it allows doubt and fear to come in. This does not allow us to live on purpose. Everyone has been new to learning something they didn't know before. Be open to receive, be bold, give yourself the opportunity to learn and grow. You will start to inspire others to live on purpose as well. It may sound odd, but the quickest way for a new situation to manifest is to make peace with your current situation. I use what I have learned, I apply it and keep moving forward. I was determined not to let my comfort zone be an invisible cage. Now when life becomes challenging it is because I am in my comfort zone or coming out of my comfort zone.

Have The Right Mindset

I am comfortable with myself and learned that I get to choose the people I want to have access to my life. I learned that I didn't have to fit in where I was meant to lead or be an example for change. We all have a different journey and purpose. I was not afraid to travel my journey and find my purpose even it if meant going alone. I learned to be grateful for all the people in my life good or not so good. I learned to see them as trainers and teachers for this journey. I extend forgiveness and gratitude in abundance. That has been the key to living the life I have always wanted. Forgive yourself and others and be grateful for the experiences. Somethings can only be learned through experience.

I learned early in my life, the less you speak, the more you hear. The more you hear, the more you understand and see things differently. I learned patterns will tell you more about a person than words could say. I learned to do the opposite of the negative things I had seen. I begin to create values, beliefs, and behaviors that were not shown around me. Creating different values, belief, and behaviors opened a space for me to be myself, love myself, and believe in myself, and this led me to my purpose.

Giving Back

As I look over my life and the things that I been through, the good and the not so good, I see the odds have always been in my favor. There isn't anything that I would do differently. From a young age, I knew I had enough strength to keep going and the ability to see things differently.

I am so proud of the little girl inside me that was so determined to have a better life. She persevered greatly so that I would become the woman I am today.

As part of my grieving from the death of Jakia, I would volunteer at schools each year. I would sponsor little girls by buying clothes, shoes, and toys. These are some of the ways it helps me to cope with the death of Jakia. I found meaning in giving back, it was to share and care for another person in the world, to understand love was not lost but shared.

When Jakia six years old she asked me to take her to Disney world, but I didn't have the money. I could not afford it being a single mom of two. Since I have been in real estate, I have been blessed to buy multiple properties near Disney world and other states. Sometimes I let friends that are single moms stay with their kids. I remember how it was for me as a single mom. It's a way to give back and hold space for someone else. I am also a business and life coach working with people to overcome life challenges, find their purpose, and other ways to create income.

When I think about the fifteen times I have moved, or the twenty-three jobs I have worked, it seems so small. It does not compare to the greatness I have now. At the age of fourteen, I always wanted my on the house now God has blessed with many houses. It was what I prayed for. I have not been a perfect person, but I have always been a praying person.

I am currently working on a teen organization. I want to create a place like I needed when I was growing up. One of the things that stood out to me the most is a saying by Joseph Campbell "find a place inside where there is joy, and the joy will burn out the pain.

Fulfill Your Purpose And Your Destiny

In the end, if you are willing to learn and grow, the odds will be in your favor too. You can find that better place if you're willing to do the work it takes to get there. You see, what is hard for us now may seem insurmountable, but the truth of the matter is this hard thing that you are going through right now is simply a lesson for your future. It is not something that is going to end you. It is something that is going to empower you and make your life better if you are willing to allow it. It takes courage to grow up and become who you are really meant to be.

I believe you can do it. Take the road less traveled. Be the person that you need to be, and then you too will find people who support you and want to be in a better place also. Surround yourself with people who will be there to support and cheer you on. Choose people who will help when following your dreams, not those who put you at risk. If family and friends are not encouraging or supporting you, that's okay extend well wishes and keep going there will be people who support you, find them and hold on. I am one of your supporters. I am cheering for you.

Sometimes it may seem like the odds are against us. It's a way to teach us something different like breaking generational cycles, create the next invention, or be a leader of change. Every challenge is a gift without challenges we would not grow. God allows new challenges to come in your life to strengthen us for the new levels of favor. Just know that you have a purpose that you need to fulfill. If you run the race with all your effort and learn and grow more and more every day, you will see that you've always been favoring your odds. The future is calling, the present is comfortable, and the past is always willing to accept you.

www.ingramcontent.com/pod-product-compliance
Lightning Source LLC
Chambersburg PA
CBHW070814220526
45466CB00002B/656